"ANYONE WHO WANTS TO GET THEIR HANDS ON THIS ANNUAL WILL HAVE TO WRESTLE IT OFF ME..."

YOUR NAME

Contents

Published 2018.
Little Brother Books Ltd, Ground Floor,
23 Southernhay East, Exeter, Devon EX1 1QL
books@littlebrotherbooks.co.uk | www.littlebrotherbooks.co.uk
Printed in Poland
The Little Brother Books trademark, email and website addresses, are the sole and exclusive properties of Little Brother Books Limited.
All WWE programming, talent names, images, likenesses, slogans, wrestling moves, trademarks, logos and copyrights are the exclusive property of WWE and its subsidiaries. All other trademarks, logos and copyrights are the property of their respective owners.

ARE YOU PUMPED... FOR WRESTLEMANIA 34?!!

"Match-packed **WrestleMania** is WWE's biggest event of the year! This year's took place at the New Orleans Superdome. 78,133 fans turned up to watch! That made it the sixth most attended *WrestleMania* in history. It hosted five nights of events: the **HALL OF FAME INDUCTION CEREMONY**, *NXT TAKEOVER*, *WRESTLEMANIA*, *MONDAY NIGHT RAW*, and *SMACKDOWN LIVE*. And guess what?

We've got all the highlights for you!"

DANIEL BRYAN

ROMAN REIGNS

JOHN CENA

BROCK LESNAR

DO YOU KNOW?

What made *WrestleMania* 2 unique, **waaay** back in 1986?

HA!

Which Superstar is a shellfish?

Prawn Strowman!

RONDA ROUSEY

There's lots to get seriously stoked about. **Six new champions** were crowned, and there were some surprise returns. **Daniel Bryan** was cleared to compete. He had to retire two years ago due to medical issues, but was crazy keen to come back. **Undertaker** also came out of retirement... to face **John Cena!** We saw the dynamic debut of **Ronda Rousey** and, er, a ten year old kid called **Nicholas!** And don't forget **Brock Lesnar** defending the WWE Universal Championship against **Roman Reigns!** Roman definitely won't forget it!

All answers on pages 76-77!

7

AJ STYLES VS.

After Shinsuke Nakamura won this year's *Royal Rumble*, what was the first thing he did? Yep, he challenged AJ Styles for the **WWE Championship!** And how did he do it? By interrupting a backstage interview with Styles to say he'd beat him at *WrestleMania*! But the WWE made Styles win the **Six Pack Challenge** at *WWE Fastlane* before he could accept. Well, success is nothing new to The Phenomenal One, and Styles came out on top yet again, defending the WWE Championship against five other guys!

**PULSE-POUNDING PROFILE:
AJ STYLES**
From: USA **Height:** 5 feet 11 inches **Weight:** 15 stone 10 pounds
Nickname: The Phenomenal One
Catchphrase: "I am phenomenal!"
Signature Moves: Phenomenal Forearm, Styles Clash, Calf Crusher

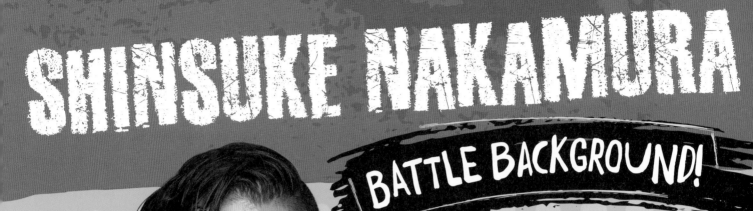

SHINSUKE NAKAMURA

BATTLE BACKGROUND!

No more delays! It was time to face Nakamura. This was truly a dream match for hardcore fans. After all, these intense rivals are **two of the world's most skilled competitors!** Ever since they joined WWE in the last few years, the WWE Universe was waiting for this moment. Sure, they'd battled around the world, but never in WWE. Ok, then? Ready for the hard fought encounter? Well, what are you waiting for? Let's go!

PULSE-POUNDING PROFILE:
SHINSUKE NAKAMURA
From: Japan **Height:** 6 feet 2 inches **Weight:** Just over 16 stone **Nickname:** King of Strong Style **Catchphrase:** "Yeaoh!"

AJ STYLES VS. SHINSUKE NAKAMURA

THE MATCH!

NAKAMURA **NAILS** THE BEST ENTRANCE, WITH ELECTRIC GUITAR AND TWO ROWS OF VIOLINISTS!

FIRST, THERE'S SOME TANGLING AGAINST THE ROPES!

THIS GOOD VIBRATIONS KICK ISN'T TOO GOOD FOR STYLES...

... **AND** THIS FLYING KICK WILL DROP HIM!

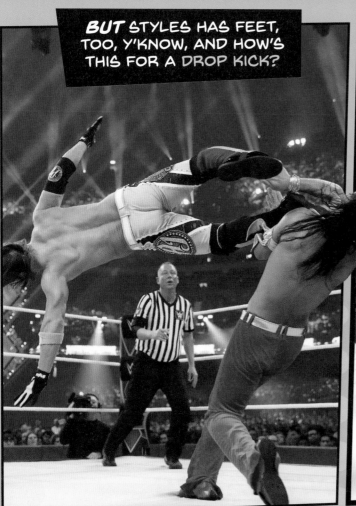

BUT STYLES HAS FEET, TOO, Y'KNOW, AND HOW'S THIS FOR A DROP KICK?

NOW HE DISHES OUT A BACKBREAKER!

BUT IT'S A STYLES CLASH THAT GETS THE FINAL PIN!

YES, STYLES WINS, AND NAKAMURA HANDS HIM THE TITLE LIKE A TRUE GENTLEMAN... THEN ATTACKS HIM AGAIN!

AWESOME ANAGRAMS!

We were so excited about *WrestleMania 34*, we got our letters mixed up! Can you rearrange these words to make them spell out the right Superstar names again? We've done the first one for you, because we're nice!

"WHICH ONE IS ME?"

"ALL I KNOW IS... ONE OF 'EM HAD BETTER BE ME!"

"ULP! OKAY, KURT, I MEAN MR. ANGLE, SIR!"

WHO ARE THESE SUPERSTARS?

1. **FINAL BORN** — FINN BALOR
2. **DARKER TUNE**
3. **CRAB SNORKEL**
4. **BOG WISH**
5. **MOANERS GRIN**
6. **SLAYS JET**
7. **SAMURAI SNAKE HUNK**
8. **LEAK GRUNT**

AND WHICH UNMISSABLE WWE EVENTS ARE THESE?

9. **DAWN SMOCK**
10. **MEATIER LAWNS**
11. **A BLURRY MOLE**

All answers on pages 76-77!

Epic Entrances!

First impressions are crucial! That's why Superstars step onto the grandest stage with style. Some even have entrances to match their skills. See if you know which of these stars made these over the top entrances!

1 Who followed an explosion by walking onto the stage through fire, then made towering flames burst from all four ring posts?

2 Who follows a funeral bell by striding through a purple haze and lightning flashes, then lifts his arms to switch on the light with a crack like thunder?

3 Who charged out, rushed to the ring with his right fist pumping, and shook the ropes with rage?

4 Who enters through golden light, under a rain of gold confetti?

5 Who came on with live violinists and a rock guitarist playing a blistering solo?

6 Who came screeching into WrestleMania 23 in a glass-shattering black Mustang car?

ULTIMATE WARRIOR

JOHN CENA

KANE

SHINSUKE NAKAMURA

UNDERTAKER

GOLDUST

All answers on pages 76-77!

ELIAS
TALKS TO US!

"

Where did you originally train for the ring... and who did you learn the most from?

I began my training in my hometown of Pittsburgh, Pennsylvania. I learned a lot from Rip Rogers and Terry Taylor, who competed during the 1980s in WWE and now works as a coach in the WWE Performance Center.

"

RIGHT NOW I NEED YOU TO SILENCE YOUR CELL PHONES, *SHUT YOUR MOUTHS* AND READ THIS INTERVIEW!

PULSE-POUNDING PROFILE:
ELIAS
From: USA Height: 6 feet 2 inches
Weight: 15 stone 4
Nicknames: The Sinister Songsmith
Catchphrase: "Walk With Elias!"
Signature Moves: Snap Swinging Neckbreaker, Rolling Cutter

"
Was there a point where you had to make a tough choice about whether to make music or sports entertainment your main career?

I always wanted to be in WWE. Even though I loved Eric Clapton and played the guitar, I never even dreamed of becoming a rock star. It just so happens that now I get to do both!

"
What music really fires you up, and what music do you wind down to?

To get fired up, my top three are AC/DC, Aerosmith and Led Zeppelin. To wind down, Clapton or Chris Stapleton.
"

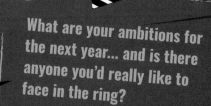

DO YOU KNOW?

What did Elias used to be known as?
THE DRIFTER
THE GRIFTER
THE LIFTER

"
What are your ambitions for the next year... and is there anyone you'd really like to face in the ring?

It would be a dream come true to face Undertaker or The Rock. I also have unfinished business with John Cena and would like to meet him again on a big stage. This year, I would like to just continue growing more and more popular. I want more people to walk with Elias than anyone could have imagined!
"

"
Who's your all-time favourite musical artist and what's the best gig you've ever been to?

Aerosmith was the best live concert I have ever seen. I've already mentioned a few others, but my all-time favorite would have to be Bruce Springsteen.
"

RONDA ROUSEY

"Former UFC champ **Ronda Rousey** was a WWE newbie. She only joined at the start of 2018! But this battle had its beginnings back in *WrestleMania 31*. **Triple H** and **Stephanie McMahon** were in the ring talkin' trash to the fans, when **The Rock** came on to interrupt them. Steph gave The Rock a slap, so he brought in audience member Ronda Rousey. She made short work of those trash talkers, placing Stephanie in an arm bar and judo-flipping Triple H! So that duo were probably still pumping for revenge three years later. Well, this was their big chance!"

Ronda found herself in a Mixed Tag Team Match for her in-ring debut. Being new to WWE, she found the perfect partner in experienced star **Kurt Angle**. How would she handle entering her first match on WWE's biggest stage? It would be cringey to lose your first ever WWE match, right? Well, hold onto your seats. You're about to find out...

PULSE-POUNDING PROFILE:
KURT ANGLE
From: USA **Height:** 6 feet 0 inches **Weight:** 15 stone 7 pounds
Nickname: Wrestling Machine
Signature moves:
Ankle Lock, Angle Slam

PULSE-POUNDING PROFILE:
RONDA ROUSEY
From: USA
Height: 5 feet 6 inches
Nickname: Rowdy
Signature Moves: Arm Bar, Samoan Drop

VS. STEPHANIE MCMAHON

AND KURT ANGLE

PULSE-POUNDING PROFILE:
STEPHANIE McMAHON
From: USA
Height: 5 feet 9 inches
Nickname: The Queen of WWE
Signature Moves:
Pedigree

PULSE-POUNDING PROFILE:
TRIPLE H
From: USA
Height: 6 feet 4 inches
Weight: 18 stone
Nickname: The Game
Signature moves:
Pedigree

AND TRIPLE H

BATTLE BACKGROUND!

RONDA ROUSEY AND KURT ANGLE
VS. STEPHANIE MCMAHON AND TRIPLE H

THE MATCH!

THEY **ALL** MEET IN THE RING... BUT WHAT'S TRIPLE H WARNING ANGLE ABOUT?

ANGLE **DISHES OUT** A BODY DROP TO TRIPLE H!

GET OUT OF **THAT**, ROUSEY -- IF YOU CAN!

ROUSEY **LAUNCHES** MCMAHON TO THE MAT!

AND SHE CAN! NOW ROUSEY APPLIES AN ARMBAR!

SHE EVEN HOISTS TRIPLE H ONTO HER SHOULDERS IN AN **INCREDIBLE** SHOW OF STRENGTH!

HA! Which Superstar do most sharks support? Finn Balor!

NOW ROUSEY SECURES **VICTORY!** MCMAHON TAPS OUT FOR THE FINISH WHEN ROUSEY GETS HER IN ANOTHER ARMBAR!

TRIPLE H GIVES ANGLE THE **PEDIGREE!** BUT ANGLE WILL SOON SEE HIM OFF BY FLIPPING HIM OVER THE TOP ROPE!

SO ROUSEY AND ANGLE WIN. WHAT AN IMPRESSIVE WWE DEBUT FOR ROUSEY!

ZOOOOOOOOO

FASTEST TITLE CHANGES!

Some Superstars lose their championships in a blink! In 2011, **Big Show** beat Mark Henry to win the **World Heavyweight Championship**. It was a brutal World Title Chairs Match. But then, in a post-match assault, Henry DDT'd him. While Big Show was lying in the ring, **Daniel Bryan** turned up to take the title. And Big Show and Bryan were supposed to be **buddies!**

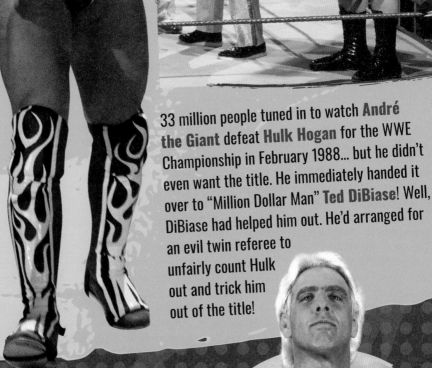

33 million people tuned in to watch **André the Giant** defeat **Hulk Hogan** for the WWE Championship in February 1988... but he didn't even want the title. He immediately handed it over to "Million Dollar Man" **Ted DiBiase!** Well, DiBiase had helped him out. He'd arranged for an evil twin referee to unfairly count Hulk out and trick him out of the title!

FASTEST RISE TO BECOME CHAMPION!

"Nature Boy" **Ric Flair** doesn't waste time. He won the 1992 *Royal Rumble* Match just 113 days after his WWE debut. That's only 16 weeks!

OM!

WWE'S FASTEST

Things can move fast in WWE! Here's proof...

FASTEST SUBMISSIONS!

At *WrestleMania* XXIV, **Kane** demolished **Chavo Guerrero** in just... wait for it... **11 seconds!** He crept up from behind, and, one quick Chokeslam later, Kane was the new *ECW* Champion!

In 2016, **The Rock** broke the *WrestleMania* record for fastest victory ever, conquering **Erick Rowan** in just **6 seconds!**

WWE'S FASTEST RISING STAR

We reckon **Elias** is WWE's fastest rising star right now. This guy introduces himself by sitting on a stool in the ring, strumming a guitar and asking "Who wants to walk with Elias?" Well, lots of people do! Elias even claims that WWE **stands** for Walks With Elias. Talk about ego! But watch out for that six-stringer. He's been known to hit other Superstars with it— especially if they interrupt one of his tunes!

JOHN CENA VS.

At first **John Cena** said he'd go to *WrestleMania* 34 as a fan only, cheering in the crowd, not competing in the ring. But then he called out **Undertaker**, saying that if the 'Deadman' turned up, he **would** be ready for him! The crowd went crazy! But Undertaker seemed to retire at *WrestleMania 33*, laying down his hat, coat and gloves in the ring. Could he really be drawn back?

PULSE-POUNDING PROFILE:
JOHN CENA
From: USA **Height:** 6 feet 1 inch
Weight: 17 stone, 9 pounds
Nickname: The Champ
Catchphrase: "You can't see me!"
Signature Moves: Attitude Adjustment, STF, Five Knuckle Shuffle.

UNDERTAKER

" Well, Taker wasn't talkin'. Cena waited week after week, but the 'Deadman' was 'dead' silent! It quickly became the most hyped match of *WrestleMania*, but it wasn't officially announced and nothing was promised! Yet fans knew there was no way this collision wouldn't happen. The only question on their minds was "Who will **win?**" Turn the page to relive the battle! "

PULSE-POUNDING PROFILE:
UNDERTAKER
From: USA **Height:** 6 feet 10 inches **Weight:** 22 stone, 7 pounds
Nickname: The Deadman
Catchphrase: "Rest in peace."
Signature moves: Tombstone, Chokeslam, Last Ride, Hell's Gate

JOHN CENA VS. UNDERTAKER

THE MATCH!

Some say it's **on!** Some say it's **off!** So will this clash of titans actually happen? We hope so, or you're gonna get four blank pages!

OUT COMES CENA, **READY** TO TAKE ON UNDERTAKER.

THE LIGHTS GO OFF, AND THE CROWD GO **CRAZY**, THINKING THE DEADMAN'S HERE! BUT WHAT'S THAT? THE STRUM OF A GUITAR?!!

I NEED YOU TO SILENCE YOUR CELL PHONES, HOLD YOUR APPLAUSE AND *SHUT YOUR MOUTHS!*

IT'S ELIAS! "WERE YOU EXPECTING **SOMEONE** ELSE?" HE ASKS. ER, YES, ACTUALLY!

ELIAS SAYS HE'S GONNA DO WHAT HE DOES BEST -- **PERFORM**. AND THAT CENA SHOULD DO WHAT HE DOES BEST -- WATCH FROM THE CROWD AS A SPECTATOR!

ELIAS GETS DOWN TO HIS TUNEFUL TROLLING. BUT CENA'S HEARD **ENOUGH** AND GETS IN THE RING!

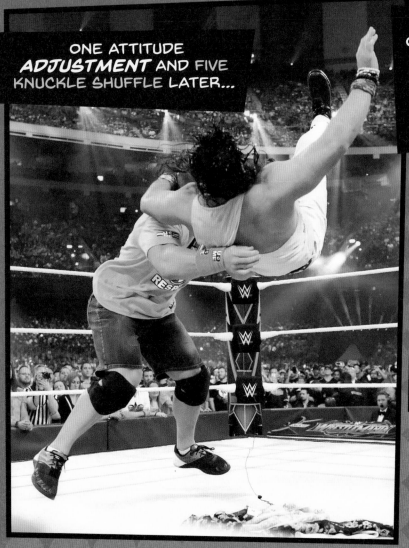

HE **SOON** GETS THE UPPER HAND ON ELIAS!

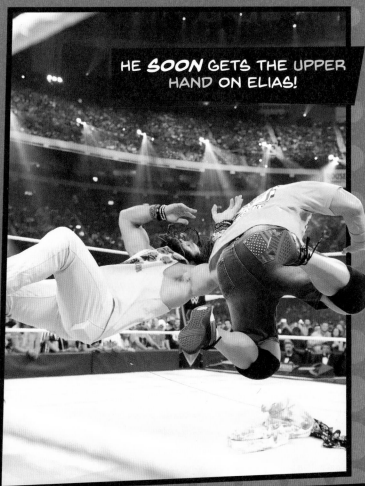

ONE ATTITUDE **ADJUSTMENT** AND FIVE KNUCKLE SHUFFLE LATER...

... AND THAT'S ONE **SINISTER** SONGSMITH WHO WON'T BE PERFORMING AN ENCORE TONIGHT!

BUT IS THAT IT? A TUSSLE WITH ELIAS BUT **NO DEADMAN?**

TURN THE PAGE, ALREADY!

JOHN CENA VS. UNDERTAKER

WOAH! THE LIGHTS GO OUT AGAIN -- AND LOOK WHAT THE SPOTLIGHT'S PICKED OUT! UNDERTAKER'S STUFF, JUST LIKE HE LEFT IT WHEN WE THOUGHT HE'D RETIRED!

THE MATCH!

NEXT MOMENT THE GEAR'S GONE -- BUT HERE COME THE FLAMES, SMOKE AND MUSIC!

YEP, THIS TIME IT'S THE **REAL DEAL!** TAKER'S BACK -- AND LOOKING FIT!

HA!

When does the WWE stage get wet?

When Roman Reigns!

FIRST, HE HITS WITH A FLYING CLOTHESLINE!

AND **HERE** COMES A FULL-FORCE BIG BOOT!

CENA SLIDES OUT OF A CHOKESLAM **AND** SLAMS TAKER...

BUT BEFORE HE CAN NAIL A FIVE KNUCKLE SHUFFLE, THE DEADMAN SITS UP! UH-OH!

UNDERTAKER GETS TO DISH OUT HIS **CHOKESLAM**, THEN SCOOPS UP CENA FOR HIS FINISHER -- A TOMBSTONE PILEDRIVER!

AND THAT LEAVES UNDERTAKER STANDING... ER, **KNEELING** TALL. HE DEMOLISHED CENA IN LESS THAN THREE MINUTES! **THE DEADMAN IS WELL AND TRULY BACK!**

SAY WHAT?!!!

We couldn't resist adding speech balloons to these fab photos!

ARE YOU SURE THIS IS HOW YOU PLAY LEAPFROG?

GROO! I'M FEELING A BIT ROPEY!

WHO LIKES MY NEW SHAWL?

NOW IT'S **YOUR** TURN!

Write a funny speech balloon for this one yourself!

ALEXA BLISS

PULSE-POUNDING PROFILE:
ALEXA BLISS
From: USA **Height:** 5 feet, 1 inch
Nickname: Little Miss Bliss
Signature Moves:
Twisted Bliss

"

This match was to contest the WWE *Raw* Women's Title. Bliss was the champion. Jax was the challenger. Now these two were former best friends. That's not to say they haven't had their ... er, difficulties! Like when Bliss won the title in 2017, defeating Sasha Banks. Jax turned up to help her celebrate, then turned on her, hitting her with an **electric chair drop**! With friends like that, you don't need enemies...

"

VS NIA JAX

BATTLE BACKGROUND!

"Not that Bliss is ideal best friend material herself! She was recently caught dissing Jax backstage at *Raw*. She said she'd only been pretending to be her best friend all along, and couldn't really stand her. She didn't realise the cameras and microphone were on, and her catty comments were being broadcast **live to the arena**! Jax witnessed it all from the stage. Guess what? She wasn't happy! So this match was set to be an intense, emotional showdown. Only one could come out on top! Let's see what happens when former friends collide..."

PULSE-POUNDING PROFILE:
NIA JAX
From: USA **Height:** 6 feet
Nickname: The Irresistible Force
Signature moves: Powerslam, Samoan Drop, Running Somersault Senton.

DO YOU KNOW?

Who won the first ever WWE Women's Elimination Chamber Match?

☐ **ALEXA BLISS**
☐ **NIA JAX**

All answers on pages 76-77!

WRESTLEMANIA

ALEXA BLISS VS. NIA JAX

THE MATCH!

FIVE-TIME WOMEN'S CHAMPION MICKIE JAMES COMES TO THE RING WITH BLISS, BUT JAX KNOCKS HER BACK OUT OF IT! THEN SHE LAYS HER OUT WITH A SAMOAN DROP!

WE GET THE BELL, AND JAX HOLDS BLISS HIGH ABOVE HER HEAD, BEFORE SENDING HER *TO THE MAT!*

BLISS GOES TO **WORK** ON JAX IN THE CORNER!

HA!

What are the WWE matches called when Superstar snails fight each other?

Hell in a shell!

SHE CAN **ONLY** KEEP HER DOWN FOR A WHILE...

BUT **MAYBE** THIS WILL DO IT. "TASTE TWISTED BLISS, NIA!"

"**YEAH?** WELL, YOU ENJOY THIS CLOTHESLINE!"

JAX **SLAMS** BLISS HARD ON THE MAT!

ALEXA BLISS **DOESN'T LOOK HAPPY** AS HER FORMER FRIEND LEAVES, HOLDING THE TITLE UP. MIND YOU, NIA JAX DOESN'T LOOK TOO HAPPY, EITHER, **BUT** SHE'S JUST GETTING EMOTIONAL 'CAUSE SHE WON! BLUB!

... BUT IT'S A SENSATIONAL **SAMOAN DROP** THAT GETS JAX THE PIN AND THE TITLE!

STUNNERS TO STRIVE FOR!

Look at the some of the beauties that WWE champions get to wrap around themselves – and swing around their heads! We've picked three of the best looking. Rate them from 1 (best) to 3 for awesomeness!

WWE INTERCONTINENTAL CHAMPIONSHIP!

YOUR RATING

WWE UNITED STATES CHAMPIONSHIP!

YOUR RATING

WWE CHAMPIONSHIP!

YOUR RATING

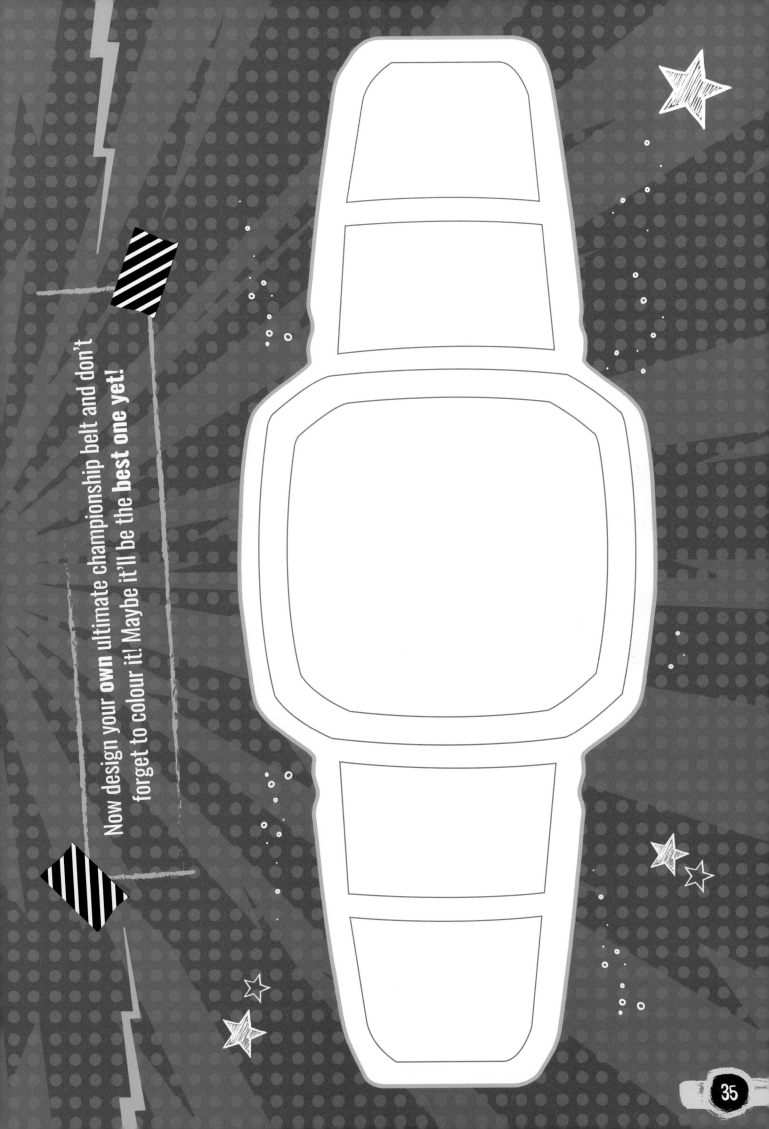

Now design your **own** ultimate championship belt and don't forget to colour it! Maybe it'll be the **best one yet!**

SUPERSTAR STATS!

Here are some more Superstar profiles for you! We've even given you the chance to add **yourself** to the roster. And why not? You'd be stacking up those Titles in no time, right?

PULSE-POUNDING PROFILE:
SETH ROLLINS
From: USA **Height:** 6 feet 1 inch
Weight: 15 stone 4 pounds
Nickname: The Architect
Signature moves: Turnbuckle Powerbomb, Curb Stomp

PULSE-POUNDING PROFILE:
THE MIZ
From: USA **Height:** 6 feet, 1 inch
Weight: 15 stone 7 pounds
Nickname: The Awesome One
Signature Moves: DDT, Skull Crushing Final

FIGHT!

SEE YOURSELF AS A SUPERSTAR?

Then fill in your own sizzling stats here – and why not add a picture?

PULSE-POUNDING PROFILE:

From: ....

Height: ....

Weight: ....

Nickname: ....

Catchphrase: ....

Signature moves: ....

....

WRESTLE-MAZE-IA!

At *WrestleMania 34*, Elias turned up in the ring, strumming his guitar, just as John Cena was expecting Undertaker! Maybe it's Cena who's hidden his six-stringer in the middle of this maze for revenge. Can you help Elias get to it and get it back?

GRRRR!

All answers on pages 76-77!

5 THINGS YOU (PROBABLY) DIDN'T KNOW ABOUT RONDA ROUSEY!

You may know that **Rowdy Ronda** was WWE's biggest signing of the year, but did you know...

Back when she was struggling to make it big, she lived in her CAR!

She's a massive POKÉMON fan!

She nearly joined the coastguard, rescuing people at sea!

She has nightmares about a ZOMBIE APOCALYPSE!

She's incredibly ticklish but says she'll go "SUPER NINJA" on you if you try tickling her. You've been warned!

So is Ronda's greatest fear a TICKLING ZOMBIE?!

ROMAN REIGNS

PULSE-POUNDING
PROFILE:
ROMAN REIGNS
From: USA **Height:** 6 feet 3
inches **Weight:** 18 stone 9 pounds
Nickname: The Big Dog
Signature Move:
Superman Punch

HA!

Which
WWE Superstar
is cold to touch
and melts in
Summer?

Big Snow!

"

Everyone had something to say
about this match – and everyone
thought they knew who'd be
standing tall at the end! They
said Lesnar would finally lose his
WWE Universal Championship
and Reigns would usher in a new
era for the title on *Raw*. Others
feared that Reigns would finally
embrace the scorn of many fans
and become a **bad guy!**

"

VS. BROCK LESNAR

BATTLE BACKGROUND!

These two sure had **history**. Lesnar defeated Reigns time after time. Reigns had been calling Lesnar a lazy part-timer for weeks, saying he didn't really care about the title. Yes, things were **personal** now, and everything seemed to be building up to a Reigns victory. Surely that would be the big end to a rivalry that was three years in the making! Wouldn't it? **Wouldn't** it??!!!

PULSE-POUNDING PROFILE:
BROCK LESNAR
From: USA **Height:** 6 feet 3 inches **Weight:** 20 stone 4 pounds
Nickname: The Beast Incarnate
Signature move: F5

ROMAN REIGNS vs. BROCK LESNAR

THE MATCH!

FIRST, LESNAR *RAMS* REIGNS BACK INTO THE CORNER TO START WORKING ON HIM!

REIGNS BREAKS *FREE* TO DELIVER A SUPERMAN PUNCH!

THEN IT'S SUPLEX CITY AS LESNAR *NAILS* ONE GERMAN SUPLEX...

...AFTER *ANOTHER!*

LESNAR **LAUNCHES** REIGNS FACE FIRST ONTO A TABLE!

NOW IT'S REIGNS'S TURN TO **SPEAR** LESNAR ONTO A TABLE!

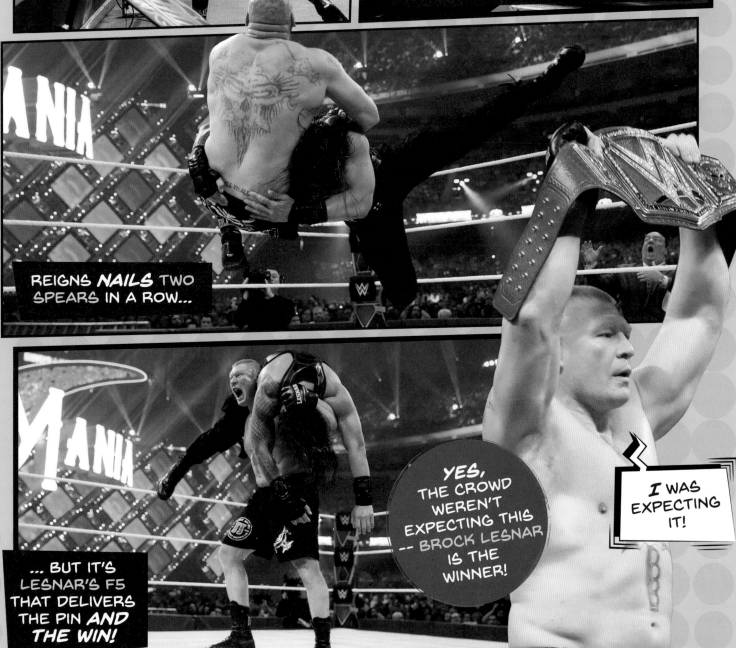

REIGNS **NAILS** TWO SPEARS IN A ROW...

... BUT IT'S LESNAR'S F5 THAT DELIVERS THE PIN **AND THE WIN!**

YES, THE CROWD WEREN'T EXPECTING THIS -- BROCK LESNAR IS THE WINNER!

I WAS EXPECTING IT!

43

JOHN CENA
TRUE OR FALSE?

No matter what he says, if you really **can't see** John Cena you must have your **eyes shut**! He's been one of WWE's biggest Superstars for over a decade! But how much do you **really** know about him? Tick whether you think the statements below are **true or false**, then check the answers at the back of the book to find out! If you get all ten right, we reckon you probably **are** John Cena!

1 WHEN HE WAS 12, JOHN ASKED FOR A WEIGHTLIFTING BENCH FOR CHRISTMAS, SO HE COULD BULK UP TO DEFEND HIMSELF FROM SCHOOL BULLIES!
○ True ○ False

2 JOHN WENT TO A PRIVATE BOARDING SCHOOL IN HIS TEENS!
○ True ○ False

U ME

3 HE WAS A STAR TENNIS PLAYER AT SCHOOL!
○ True ○ False

4 HE TRIED TO BECOME A COP — BUT FAILED THE EXAM!
○ True ○ False

5 BEFORE HE WAS FAMOUS, HE HAD A JOB CLEANING TOILETS!
○ True ○ False

COMPETITION WINNERS

Following last year's collaboration Delzinski, Little Brother Books and WWE teamed up to run an even BIGGER competition. This year we wanted you to create your very own WWE Championship in WWE Games - WWE 2K18!

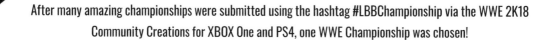

The winning creation received a WWE Champion and is featured in this year's WWE Annual!

After many amazing championships were submitted using the hashtag #LBBChampionship via the WWE 2K18 Community Creations for XBOX One and PS4, one WWE Championship was chosen!

WWE Championship was created by Usmaan Ali

Also, congratulations to both Matt Baker And Neale Maker
two awesome runners up!

DELZINSKI

Name:
Delzinski
YouTube Channel: YouTube.com/VintageShizzle
Website: Delzinski.com
Twitter: @Delzinski
Instagram @Delzinski
Facebook: Facebook.com/Delzinski

SURVIVOR SERIES

@DELZINSKI @DELZINSKI

NO MERCY

@DELZINSKI @DELZINSKI

HELL IN A CELL

ABOUT ME

Delinzinski's YouTube channel has 98,000+ subscribers and 30+ million video views! His Universe Mode series lets him take control of WWE. Who wouldn't want **that** kind of power?! He plays out his dream storylines and matches, but he doesn't go too crazy. He tries to keep things realistic, so it feels authentic!

His storylines are made to thrill! How about Roman Reigns turning on the fans and becoming The Rock's rival? Or Jeff Hardy challenging Brock Lesnar for the WWE Championship? Or The NWO returning with Drew McIntyre as their leader? It's like slipping into an alternate WWE reality!

Check out Delzinski's WWE Universe Mode with the YouTube channel link above. We're just worried you won't want to come back!

DID YOU KNOW?

Delzinski's favourite match of all time is from WrestleMania 25, when **Shawn Michaels** attempted to defeat the Undertakers streak!

EXCLUSIVE INTERVIEW!

CHARLOTTE

TALKS TO US!

"

With (wrestling manager and retired WWE Superstar) Ric Flair as your dad, were you strongly encouraged to follow your WWE ambitions... or did he ever advise you *against* it?

My Dad never advised me against it. He knew wrestling would be something I would be good at, but because I had never shown an interest or passion for it, he was shocked when I decided to try out for NXT. Not until my NXT Championship match with Natalya did he start to understand how serious I was and how competitive the Women's Division was.

"

Who were *your* female role models? Were they famous or people you knew?

My female role models growing up were my coaches. After I graduated college, the older women I trained as a personal trainer became mentors. Then once I started wrestling, Stephanie McMahon, Natalya and the other Four Horsewomen were people who I looked up to and wanted to learn from.

DO YOU KNOW?

Charlotte was born in a city called Charlotte!

TRUE or FALSE?

You had an accidental gash during your *WrestleMania* match, which looked painful. How do you cope with something like that, or was the adrenalin pumping so much in the ring that you didn't even notice it?

My adrenaline was pumping so much that I didn't even realize it until I got backstage and took a moment to breathe. When I am in the moment, one that will be remembered for the rest of my life, nothing is going to take me out of the zone. Asuka pushed me harder than I've ever been. It was an honour facing her.

Charlotte Flair

CHARLOTTE'S RIGHT!

They were rare, but there **were** female gladiators in Ancient Rome. They were called gladiatrices or Amazons (after the mythical warrior women of Ancient Greece!).

Congratulations on defeating Asuka at *WrestleMania*. Your gold bathed entrance was amazing! If you could visit any period in history would it *be* the time of centurions and gladiators?

Yes. Female Gladiators fought just as hard while displaying beauty, strength, grace and passion during the Roman Games.

All answers on pages 76-77!

HARD-HITTING HIGHLIGHTS!

Behold more breathtaking best bits... from WrestleMania 34!

TRIPLE THREAT THRILLS!

A wild match between three world champs opened WrestleMania 34! The **Intercontinental Championship** pitted **The Miz**, **Seth Rollins** and **Finn Bálor** against each other. How's that for a contrast of combat styles? Of course, The Miz was desperate to retain his championship...

And, sure, he killed in the first third, dishing out a DDT to Rollins, and tying up Bálor in a Figure Four Leglock! But he couldn't keep it up...

It looked like Bálor might win for a while... until Rollins hit a Stomp on him while he was rolling Miz over! Rollins was the winner, and soon he was swinging the championship around his head like a lasso! Welcome to the world of **Grand Slam Champions**, Seth – you've now won **every major WWE title** there is!

50

THE EMPRESS OF TOMORROW'S WINNING STREAK... ENDS TODAY!

Charlotte Flair made one of the event's best entrances, showered in gold and flanked by her personal gladiators! Four years ago in this same building, she played a similar role in Triple H's entrance!

Flair also made WWE history when – shocker! – she became the first one to beat Japanese star **Asuka's** unbeaten streak. When Flair locked in her Figure-Eight Leg Lock, the Empress of Tomorrow was forced to tap. That amazed the crowd... some of whom were breathless from this instant classic!

FATAL 4-WAY!

The **WWE United States Championship Match** pitted defending champ **Randy Orton, Jinder Mahal, Rusev** and **Bobby Roode** against each other. Rusev was a fan favourite to win, and he did take control at one point... but not for long!

AND THE WINNER WAS...
Jinder Mahal!

WRESTLEMANIA'S 10 YEAR OLD CHAMPION!

One of *WrestleMania's* weirdest moments was every WWE kid fan's dream! **Braun Strowman** had been looking for a partner for weeks to take on Sheamus and Cesaro. On the night, he told the crowd "My partner... is one of you!" Then the Monster Among Men picked out a 10 year old boy named **Nicholas** to be his partner competing for the *Raw* Tag Team Titles... and they won!

WHAT NEXT?
Nicholas vs. Brock Lesnar for WrestleMania 35?!!

PUZZLE BREAK!

How many words can you make from the letters of

WRESTLEMANIA ...?

Believe it or not, **over 1,500 words are possible!** They include little ones like 'tin' and 'tar', bigger ones like 'wrist' and 'sweat', and even longer ones like 'terminals' and 'materials.'

See how many you can make in just ten minutes! Time yourself, and remember – you can only use each one of the 12 letters once!

SIGNATURE MOVES

Real or Fake?

WWE Superstars are famous for dishing out cool moves! We've listed some of their famous **signature moves** right here. We've also put in six total **fakes** we know no Superstar has ever done... because we've just **made 'em up!** Do you know your WWE well enough to say which of these **aren't** genuine?

Prove it! Tick the fakes...

GO TO SLEEP ☐

FROG SPLASH ☐

CAMEL CLUTCH ☐

CRAB CLAMP ☐

CURBSTOMP ☐

LIONSAULT ☐

RHINO CHARGE POWERSLAM ☐

LAST RIDE ☐

WHISPER IN THE WIND ☐

SERPENT STING TAKEDOWN ☐

TWIST OF FATE ☐

SIDEWALK SHOVEL ☐

ROCK BOTTOM ☐

ALLIGATOR EARTHQUAKE ☐

SPINAROONIE ☐

All answers on pages 76-77!

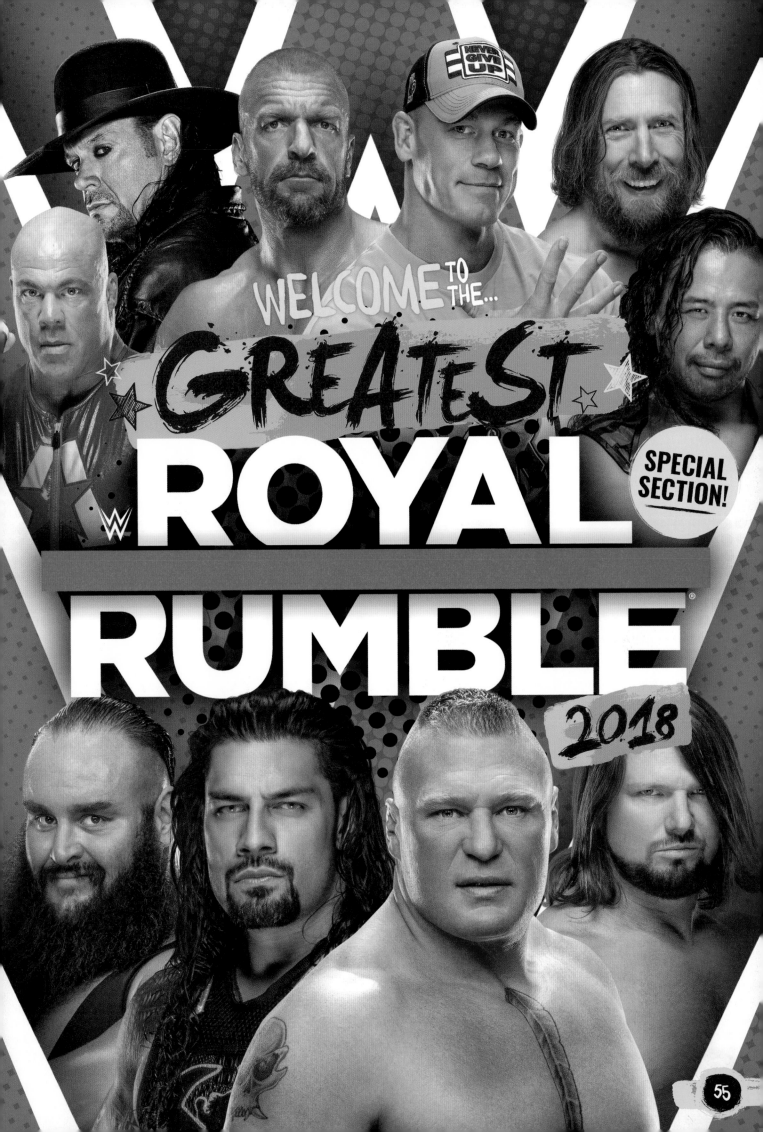

WELCOME TO THE...

GREATEST

ROYAL

RUMBLE

2018

SPECIAL SECTION!

NEVER GIVE UP

55

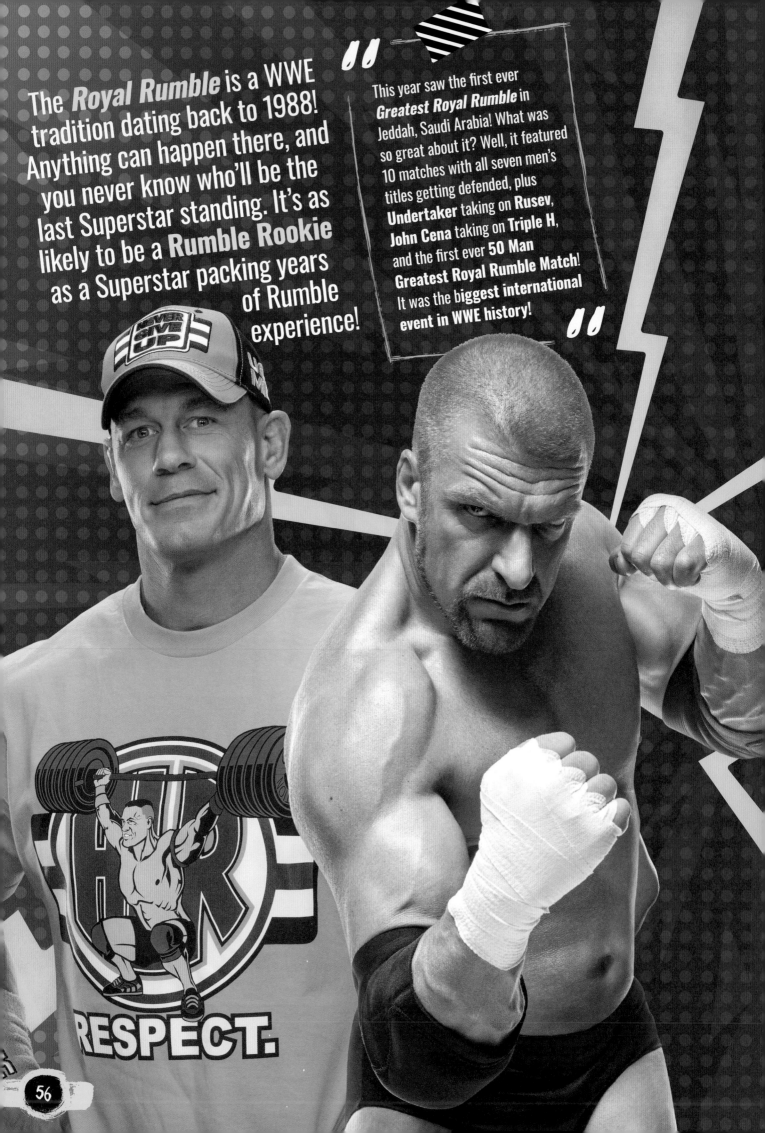

The **Royal Rumble** is a WWE tradition dating back to 1988! Anything can happen there, and you never know who'll be the last Superstar standing. It's as likely to be a **Rumble Rookie** as a Superstar packing years of Rumble experience!

" This year saw the first ever **Greatest Royal Rumble** in Jeddah, Saudi Arabia! What was so great about it? Well, it featured 10 matches with all seven men's titles getting defended, plus **Undertaker** taking on **Rusev**, **John Cena** taking on **Triple H**, and the first ever **50 Man Greatest Royal Rumble Match**! It was the biggest international event in WWE history! "

RESPECT.

ROYAL RUMBLE RECORDS!

Santino Marella spent the shortest time in a single *Royal Rumble*. He lasted just **1.9 seconds**. It was hardly worth him turning up!

Steve Austin has won the most *Royal Rumble* Matches – 3!

Kane holds the record for entering the **most** *Royal Rumble* matches. He entered **19**. Pity he never got around to winning one!

One of the greatest victories was **Rey Mysterio's** in 2006, when he stayed in the ring for 62 minutes and 12 seconds! Only four other Superstars had stayed in the ring for over an hour before, and none of them for **that** long!

DiD YOU KNOW?

Nearly one third of *Royal Rumble* winners won on their **first ever appearance**, including Brock Lesnar in 2003. So much for experience!

It's a tradition that the *Royal Rumble* Match winner earns a **World Title** match at *WrestleMania*... so there's plenty at stake!

SPOT THE DIFFERENCE!

As if there wasn't already enough to look at in the 50 Man *Royal Rumble*, we've altered some details on the second pic. Unlike the Superstars' muscles, the 10 differences are only small. See how many you can spot!

All answers on pages 76-77!

50 MAN ROYAL RUMBLE WORD SEARCH!

You'll find some of the Superstars who took part in this mega-battle in the grid below. We've hidden their names every which way we can: horizontally, diagonally, vertically and even backwards! Try to find as many as you can in less than 50 minutes. It's tricky but, believe us, FINDING them is easier than FIGHTING them!

```
D T H E M I Z P F S I U E B N
P A X R Z C R U J L K C R R O
R S N E I O M E P V W O N O T
F V G I P J F P J D M A I C R
E N I G E F L D P A M A W K O
F G Q Q H L W E N W T J O L Y
B Y I A D K B R O S G M H E D
C H R I S J E R I C H O S S N
O D N Y O I T T Y C Y Y G N A
Y D Y S G S A P L A K P I A R
M F I N N B A L O R N A B R R
L C S U L A H A M R E D N I J
O P A E O J A O M A S H F E T
U R V H S O R Q J V F B Z N B
B X O Y S U W K H E H J Y Z D
```

HERE'S WHO TO LOOK FOR!

Daniel Bryan Braun Strowman   Samoa Joe Chris Jericho
Randy Orton Finn Balor Jeff Hardy Kane Brock Lesnar Roman Reigns
Big Show The Miz Batista Jinder Mahal

All answers on pages 76-77!

And the Winners are...

These Superstars stood tall after some of the Greatest Royal Rumble's biggest battles...

John Cena broke his big match losing streak to top **Triple H**, dishing out **three Attitude Adjustments!** Before Cena finally pinned Triple H, **both** legends taunted each other by stealing each others moves!

DID YOU KNOW?

Cena and Triple H also met in the main event of *WrestleMania 22!*

> At one point, Rusev was removed from his planned casket match with Undertaker, to be replaced with Chris Jericho. Then he was back in, vowing to "bury the Undertaker in the sands of Saudi Arabia." Bold words! But even though he had help from Aiden English, Undertaker managed to shut both Superstars inside the casket!

Roman Reigns was pitted against Brock Lesnar for a Universal Championship rematch... inside a steel cage! Lesnar delivered three suplexes and some F-5s, and Reigns dished out Superman Punches and a Powerbomb in return. Reigns finally speared Lesnar through the cage wall, and both men hit the floor.

" Lesnar was declared the winner for hitting it first, but replays suggest that Reigns should have won. Well, it's about time, right? Of course, he had a Greatest Royal Grumble about it. As far as he's concerned, he did win! So must these Superstars fight again... or should Reigns just stay away from Lesnar for a while? "

PUZZLE BREAK!

Who has the most Rumble eliminations overall?

☐ *Kane*   ☐ *Roman Reigns*

All answers on pages 76-77!

THE 50 MAN ROYAL RUMBLE

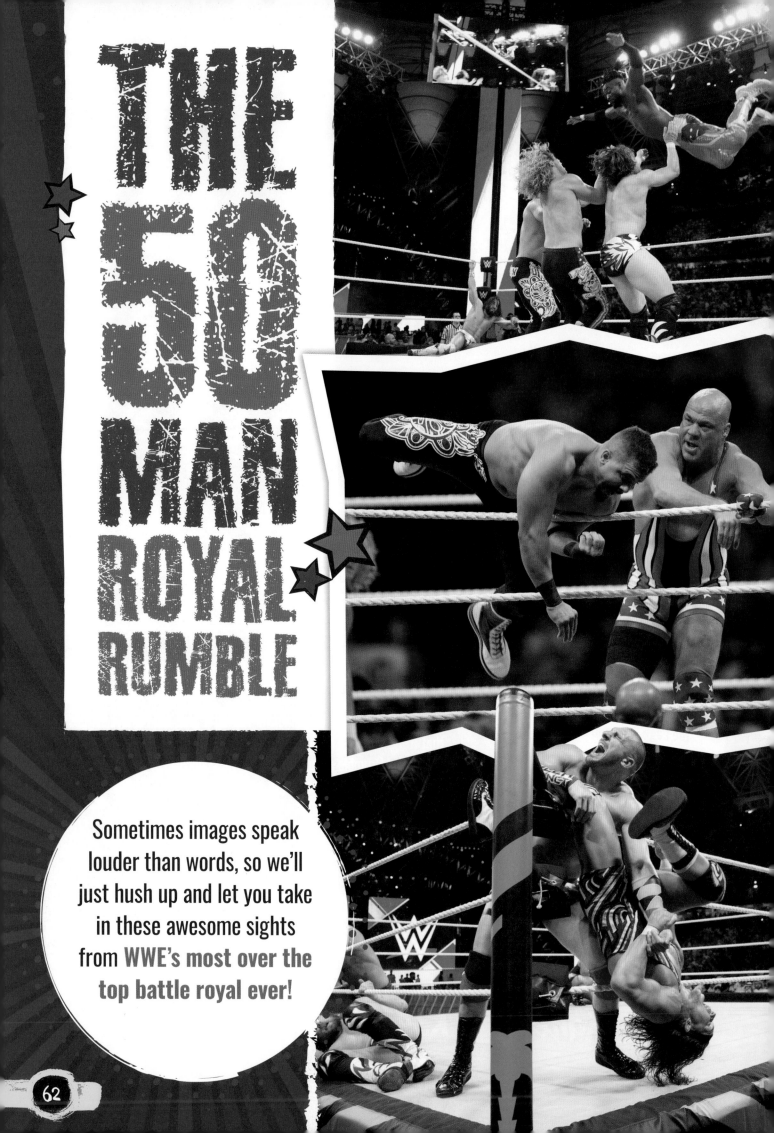

Sometimes images speak louder than words, so we'll just hush up and let you take in these awesome sights from **WWE's most over the top battle royal ever!**

Titus O' Neil had an **epic fail** with an **epic fall!** He ran on in the match's Number 39 slot, but accidentally tripped over and slid under the ring!

Finally, it was down to just **Braun Strowman** and **Big Cass!** After a short struggle, the Monster Among Men eliminated Cass and made history as the **first ever winner** of the 50 Man *Royal Rumble*! That's a **monster career peak** for Strowman!

WERE YOU PAYING ATTENTION?

Let's see! Answer the questions below without turning back the pages, and find out how much of a *Greatest Royal Rumble* expert you are!

1 IN **WHICH COUNTRY** DID THE GREATEST *ROYAL RUMBLE* TAKE PLACE?

2 WHO WON THE **JOHN CENA** vs. **TRIPLE H** MATCH?

3 WHO DID **UNDERTAKER** SHUT IN A CASKET?

4 WHO WAS DECLARED **WINNER** OF THE STEEL CAGE MATCH?

5 WHO **WON** THE 50 MAN *ROYAL RUMBLE*?

POW!

6 WHO HAD AN **EPIC FALL** AND SLID UNDER THE RING?

All answers on pages 76-77!

REMEMBERING
BRUNO SAMMARTINO
1935 - 2018

He paved the way for the stars of today!

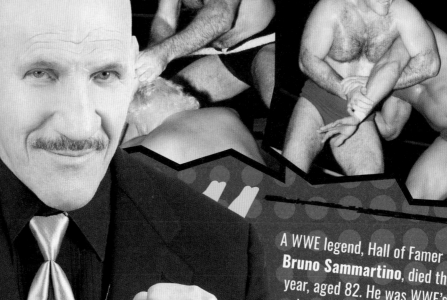

A WWE legend, Hall of Famer **Bruno Sammartino**, died this year, aged 82. He was WWE's ultimate star for nearly 20 years, and its longest reigning champion – for an amazing 2,803 consecutive days. That's nearly eight years! He was WWE's ultimate good guy, and a hero to millions of fans. He stopped competing in the early 1980s. Arnold Schwarzenegger inducted him into the WWE Hall of Fame in 2013.

DID YOU KNOW?
Sammartino was John Cena's dad's favourite performer – and his grandad's favourite, too!

WWE'S YOUNGEST EVER CHAMPIONS!

Ever get frustrated that you're too young to be a WWE Champion yourself? Well, you don't need to be **that** old, and these guys prove it! Maybe you won't have to wait too long after all...

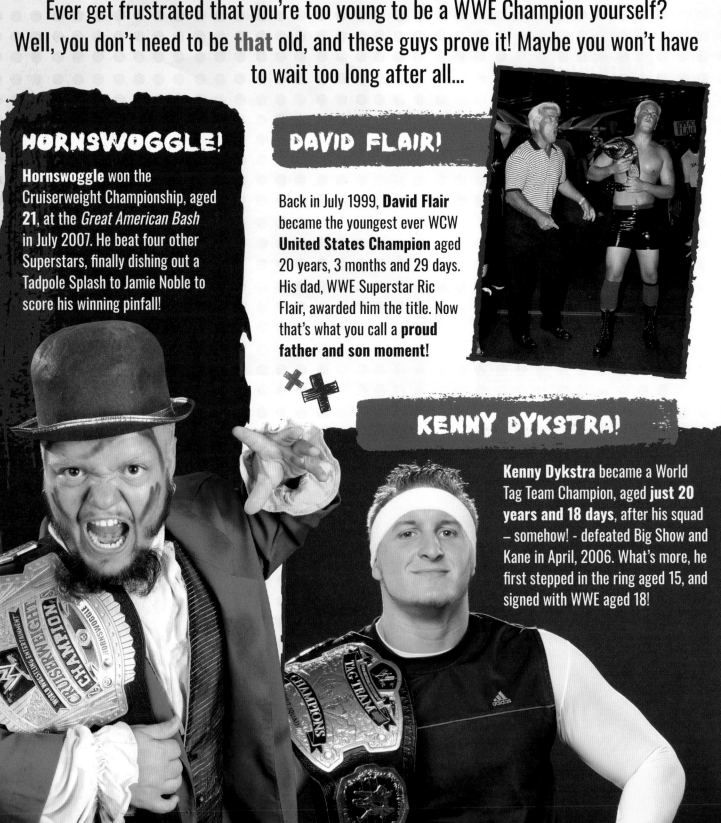

HORNSWOGGLE!

Hornswoggle won the Cruiserweight Championship, aged **21**, at the *Great American Bash* in July 2007. He beat four other Superstars, finally dishing out a Tadpole Splash to Jamie Noble to score his winning pinfall!

DAVID FLAIR!

Back in July 1999, **David Flair** became the youngest ever WCW **United States Champion** aged 20 years, 3 months and 29 days. His dad, WWE Superstar Ric Flair, awarded him the title. Now that's what you call a **proud father and son moment!**

KENNY DYKSTRA!

Kenny Dykstra became a World Tag Team Champion, aged **just 20 years and 18 days**, after his squad – somehow! - defeated Big Show and Kane in April, 2006. What's more, he first stepped in the ring aged 15, and signed with WWE aged 18!

TYLER BATE!

Tyler Bate made history in January 2017, when he became the first ever WWE United Kingdom Champion. He was just **19 years, 10 months** and **8 days** old!

RENE DUPREE!

René Duprée was a World Tag Team title winner on June 15th, 2003, aged just **19 years and six months**! He was the first ever teen titan to hold a championship in the history of WWE... and the universe! He won another Tag Team Title the next year, too, aged 20.

NICHOLAS!

10 year old **Nicholas** was handpicked from the crowd by Brawn Strowman, as his mystery partner for *WrestleMania* 34's tag team match. The Monster did all the hard work, but Nicholas still shared the championship title. They relinquished the titles after one night. Well, Nicholas had to get back to his schoolwork!

All answers on pages 76-77!

PUZZLE BREAK!

TRUE OR FALSE?

Tyler Bate is vegan – meaning he doesn't eat any meat or dairy products, or wear any animal products.

☐ TRUE ☐ FALSE

WWE HALL OF

The **WWE Hall of Fame Induction** Ceremony was held the Friday before *WrestleMania 34*. It's an annual event to celebrate Legends who've made a lasting mark on sports entertainment!

FORMER SUPERSTARS WHO'VE BEEN INDUCTED INCLUDE...

1

2

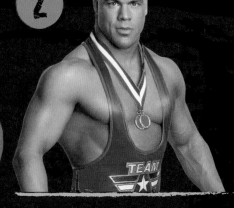

3

ANDRE THE GIANT!
This larger than life Superstar, who died in 1993, was the first **ever Hall** of Fame inductee!

KURT ANGLE!
He was **a four time World Champion** over seven years with WWE! John Cena inducted him in 2017.

RIC FLAIR!
This Superstar had **16 World Title reigns**! No **wonder** he's in the Hall of Fame!

Here are some of the reasons why fans love the ceremony...

> MANY SUPERSTARS SHED THEIR CHARACTERS AND SHOW THEIR REAL SELVES!

> SUPERSTARS GET AS MUCH TIME AS THEY NEED TO TELL THEIR STORIES PROPERLY! (WELL, WHO'D DARE TO INTERRUPT THEM?!)

> THERE ARE LOTS OF LAUGHS, GOOD STORIES AND MEMORABLE MOMENTS -- WE HOPE!

And when it kicks off like this, you know it'll be no **ordinary** awards ceremony...

TASTE TABLE, DUDE! NO-ONE TELLS US TO **WRAP UP OUR SPEECH!**

SORRY, DUDLEY BOYZ! TALK FOR AS LONG AS YOU LIKE!

SO LET'S SEE WHO TURNED UP TO BE INDUCTED (IN OTHER WORDS, 'BE INTRODUCED INTO') THE CLASS OF 2018 ...

FAME 2018!

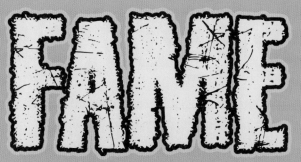

THE DUDLEY BOYZ!
The multi-decorated tag team poked fun at people, then slammed a stagehand through a table!

IVORY!
The former WWE Women's Champion was inducted by her rival Molly Holly!

HILLBILLY JIM!
He came out dancing and gave a humble acceptance speech!

KID ROCK!
This singer was this year's **celebrity** inductee. He wrote Undertaker's entrance song, but it was Triple H who inducted him!

MARK HENRY!
The World's Strongest Man was inducted by his old tag team partner Big Show!

JEFF JARRETT!
This **six-time Intercontinental Champ** got all emotional!

JARRIUS "JJ" ROBERTSON!
15 year old Jarrius won The Warrior Award. Two liver transplants helped to save his life. He told fans to stop booing his buddy Roman Reigns!

GOLDBERG!
This Superstar had a **173 match unbeaten streak**! Tonight he was the headline act, and thanked lots of people. It reminds you that getting to the top is truly a **team effort**!

HA!

Which TV show do lions like best?
WWE ROAR!

This year's ceremony ran for **four** and a half hours! Let's hope no-one missed the last bus home!

NICKNAMES CROSSWORD!

Do you know the WWE Superstars by their **nicknames?** We've used some famous ones for our crossword clues. Now you just need to write the stars' names in the boxes! We've filled in **10 Across** to get you going, and a few other boxes, too. Not 100% sure how to spell every name correctly? Just flick through the book, find 'em and check!

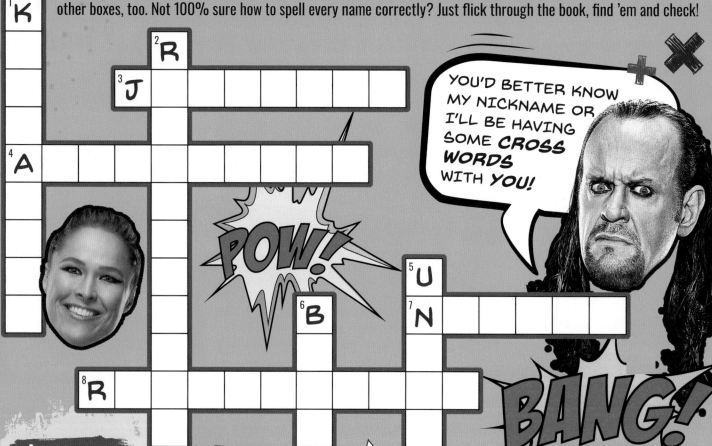

YOU'D BETTER KNOW MY NICKNAME OR I'LL BE HAVING SOME **CROSS WORDS** WITH **YOU!**

POW!

BANG!

Across

3. The Champ
4. Little Miss Bliss
7. The Irresistible Force
8. Rowdy
9. The Phenomenal One
10. The Game

Down

1. Wrestling Machine
2. The Big Dog
5. The Deadman
6. The Beast Incarnate

IN **MY** OPINION, 6 DOWN IS THE **BEST** SUPERSTAR EVER!

DO YOU KNOW?
What does **Triple H** stand for?

All answers on pages 76-77!

BIG SCREEN SUPERSTARS!

Some WWE Superstars switch between the ring and the big screen! Do you know which movies the Superstars below appear in? Follow the lines to check if you're right!

THE MIZ

BATISTA

TRIPLE H

DWAYNE 'THE ROCK' JOHNSON

AVENGERS: INFINITY WAR

THE CHAPERONE

SANTA'S LITTLE HELPER

RAMPAGE

All answers on pages 76-77!

THEEEEEEY'

It's always a thrill when old favourites return to WWE as active competitors, and this year saw some major returns! You've already read about Undertaker, so now let's turn to these two titans...

DANIEL BRYAN!

Former World Champion Daniel Bryan's return was a shocker, coming straight out of nowhere! He said farewell to the WWE Universe as an in-ring competitor back in 2016. He'd suffered serious injuries, and no-one wanted that to happen again. So fans were just getting used to the idea that they'd never see him compete in a WWE ring again... ever! Next thing, they were getting stoked about his **return match** at *WrestleMania 34*...

"Yes, doctors had cleared the bearded bulldog to compete again – and he didn't disappoint! He had a **Tag Team win** alongside Shane McMahon, defeating Sam Zayn and Kevin Owens. And you know what? It looked like he'd never been away! Now everyone's talking about the potential dream matches they want to see him take part in!"

RE BACK!!!

What do Elias's parrot fans do?

Squawk with Elias!

"**Bobby Lashley** returned to WWE in April 2018, interrupting one of Elias's rude concerts in the *Monday Night Raw* ring! The crowd went crazy, chanting "Welcome back". Then they gasped at the sheer power on display as Lashley hoisted Elias into the air... for ages... before destroying him with a Standing Suplex!"

BOBBY LASHLEY!

"Yes, this human wrecking ball is back, and he says he's in for "the big matches." But why now? "Unfinished business," he says. Not only that, but he reckons he's become a much more complete Superstar in his time away, and he wants to show the WWE Universe how much he's improved. We aren't about to argue... but **Braun Strowman** still toppled him at the *Greatest Royal Rumble's* 50 man battle!"

WHAT'S COMING UP... IN 2019!

WWE gets bigger every year, and guess what? That's not about to stop in 2019! Here's just some of what you can start getting excited about...

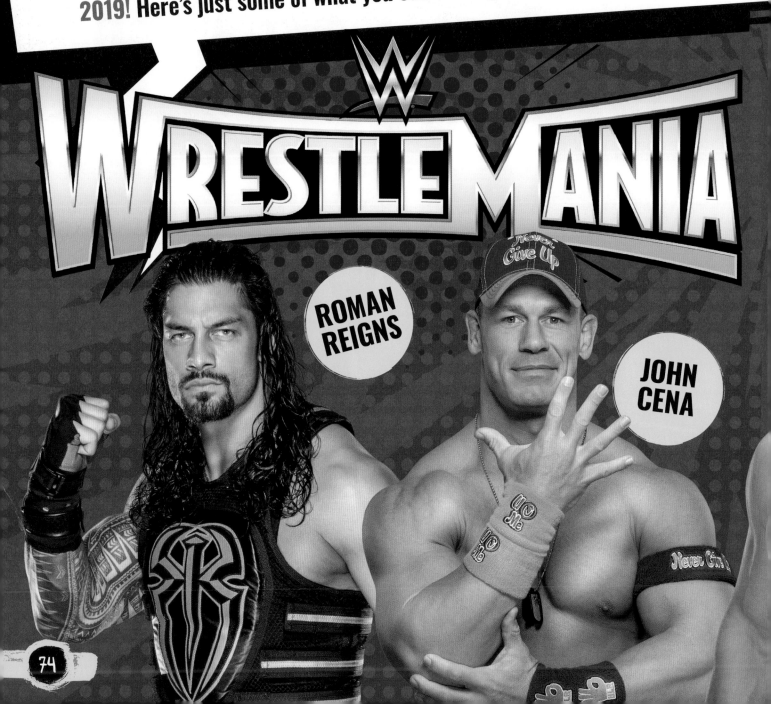

ROMAN REIGNS

JOHN CENA

The **Royal Rumble** takes place on January 27th, in Chase Field baseball stadium in Phoenix, Arizona, USA. Over

40,000 FANS

are expected to show!

There'll also be a **WWE NXT Takeover** event the day before in Phoenix's Talking Stick Resort Arena. How's that for an awesome weekend?

ROYAL RUMBLE

WrestleMania will return to MetLife Stadium in New Jersey, USA, for the first time since 2013. (That's when John Cena defeated The Rock to win the WWE Championship, and Undertaker overcame CM Punk!) It's usually home to football teams the New York Giants and the New York Jets, but on Sunday, April 7th forget football, it'll be devoted to *Wrestlemania 35!*

There'll also be four nights of events at nearby Brooklyn's Barclays Centre, including the Hall of Fame ceremony, *NXT Takeover*, *Monday Night Raw* and *SmackDown Live!* As if living in New York wasn't cool enough already!

MARK THOSE DATES IN YOUR DIARIES AND ON YOUR CALENDARS, FANS. IF YOU MISS 'EM, YOU'LL BE KICKING YOURSELF NAKAMURA-STYLE!

BROCK LESNAR

RONDA ROUSEY

DANIEL BRYAN

ANSWERS

PAGE 7

It's the only WrestleMania to take place on a Monday, instead of starting on Sunday!

PAGE 12

AWESOME ANAGRAMS
1. FINN BALOR
2. UNDERTAKER
3. BROCK LESNAR
4. BIG SHOW
5. ROMAN REIGNS
6. A. J. STYLES
7. SHINSUKE NAKAMURA
8. KURT ANGLE
9. SMACKDOWN
10. WRESTLEMANIA
11. ROYAL RUMBLE

PAGE 13

EPIC ENTRANCES
BOX 1: KANE.
BOX 2: UNDERTAKER.
BOX 3: ULTIMATE WARRIOR.
BOX 4: GOLDUST.
BOX 5: SHINSUKE NAKAMURA.
BOX 6: JOHN CENA.

PAGE 14-15

ELIAS EXCLUSIVE INTERVIEW

DO YOU KNOW? THE DRIFTER

PAGE 30-31

ALEXA BLISS VS NIA JAX BATTLE BACKGROUND
QUIZ BOX: ALEXA BLISS

PAGE 38-39

PAGE 44-45

JOHN CENA TRUE OR FALSE

1. TRUE 2. TRUE 3. FALSE 4. TRUE 5. TRUE 6. TRUE
7. FALSE – Kurt won! 8. FALSE 9. TRUE 10. TRUE

PAGE 48-49

CHARLOTTE FLAIR EXCLUSIVE INTERVIEW
DO YOU KNOW? TRUE

PAGE 54

SIGNATURE MOVES

The fake moves were CRAB CLAMP, RHINO CHARGE POWERSLAM, SERPENT STING TAKEDOWN, SIDEWALK SHOVEL and ALLIGATOR EARTHQUAKE.

SPOT THE DIFFERENCE

WORDSEARCH

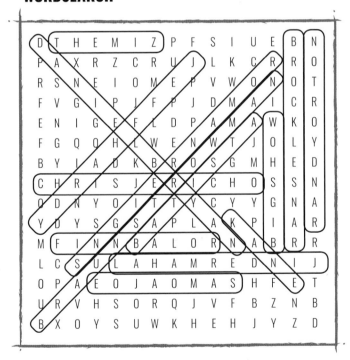

AND THE WINNERS ARE...

PUZZLE BREAK: KANE!

WERE YOU PAYING ATTENTION?

1. Saudi Arabia 2. John Cena 3. Rusev and Aiden English
4. Brock Lesnar 5. Brawn Strowman 6. Titus O'Neil

YOUNGEST EVER CHAMPIONS!

PUZZLE BOX: TRUE!

CROSSWORD

PUZZLE BOX: Hunter Hearst Hemsley, his original ring name!

BIG SCREEN SUPERSTARS

Dwayne 'The Rock' Johnson – Rampage, Batista – Avengers Infinity War, The Miz – Santa's Little Helper, Triple H – The Chaperone.